# MODERN CHINA

## BY ALDEN R. CARTER

PHOTOGRAPHS OF CHINA TODAY BY
CAROL S. AND ALDEN R. CARTER

FRANKLIN WATTS   A FIRST BOOK   1986
NEW YORK   LONDON   TORONTO   SYDNEY

Many thanks to all who helped with
*Modern China*, especially my agent Ray Puechner,
my editor Marjory Kline, and my friends
Sue Babcock, Dean Markwardt, and Dale Yakaites.
I am particularly indebted to Dr. David Chang
of the University of Wisconsin–Oshkosh for
his advice, expertise, and unfailing good humor.
As always, my wife Carol was my greatest support.
This book is for our friends and
traveling companions Don and Georgette Beyer.

Map by Vantage Art

Photographs on pp. 22 and 26
courtesy of The Bettmann Archive.

Library of Congress Cataloging in Publication Data

Carter, Alden R.
Modern China.
(A First book)

Bibliography: p.
Includes index.
Summary: Examines the history, daily life, customs,
education, work, and recreation of modern China.
1. China—Juvenile literature. [1. China]
I. Carter, Carol S., ill. II. Title.
DS706.C35   1986          951.05          85-26336
ISBN 0-531-10124-X

# CONTENTS

# MODERN
# CHINA

Chinese words in this book are spelled according to the Pinyin system for the Romanization of Chinese words. The Pinyin system was adopted by the State Council of the People's Republic of China in 1979 to replace the Wade/Giles system developed in Great Britain in the nineteenth century. Although Chinese is a tonal language very unlike English, the pronunciation of most Chinese words can be approximated by using the equivalent English sounds for the letters in the Pinyin spellings. For the more difficult words, a pronunciation aid has been added in brackets.

# INTRODUCTION

At Yichang [ee-chan] in Central China, a great dam is rising to harness the power of one of the world's mightiest rivers, the Yangtze [yan-tze]. Work on the structure goes on twenty-four hours a day, seven days a week. When it is completed in 1986, the dam will rank as one of the world's largest, fully three times the size of America's Hoover Dam. Then the forty thousand construction workers will move upstream to start an even more colossal dam.

With each day the face of China is changing. Hundreds of millions of Chinese are laboring to build the China of the future. The obstacles they face are immense. The most populous nation on earth is still recovering from years of turmoil. Several neighboring countries, particularly the USSR, are unfriendly. There is a lack of modern technology—even such basics as trucks and tractors. Population growth threatens to overwhelm China's resources. Still, if China fails in its push to become a modern nation, it will not be for lack of muscle, brains, and sacrifice on the part of the Chinese people.

# I

## CHINA: MOST POPULOUS NATION ON EARTH

The population of China is huge. More than a billion people, roughly one out of every four people on earth, live in the People's Republic of China. This population is both the nation's greatest strength and its greatest weakness.

Because of the scarcity of modern technology, many hands are needed to do the work in China. Eighty percent of the people live in rural areas, the vast majority working as farmers. (In the United States fewer than three people in a hundred are farmers.) But if the population continues to grow, the best efforts of these hundreds of millions of farmers may not be enough. China may simply run out of farmland and food. Population control is one of the major problems facing the most populous nation on earth.

### THE PEOPLE OF CHINA

Over ninety percent of the Chinese are Han. Most Han Chinese are shorter and slighter than the average person in

Western nations such as the United States, but there are also many tall and big-boned people. Although almost all Han Chinese have brown eyes and straight black hair, skin coloring and facial features vary widely. The old myth about the Chinese all looking the same is simply untrue.

The Han Chinese share a common language, but how it is spoken changes from region to region. These regional variations are called dialects, and a speaker of one dialect may have difficulty understanding a speaker of another. Fortunately, written Chinese is universal. It is not uncommon to see two people from different areas of the country rapidly sketching Chinese language characters to overcome a breakdown in verbal communication.

In addition to the Han majority, some sixty minorities live in the People's Republic. Some minorities number only a few thousand, while others have millions of members. Most of the minorities make their homes in the vast, sparsely populated western and northwestern regions of China. The hardy Tibetans live "on the roof of the world"—a high plateau north of the Himalayas, the tallest mountain range in the world. Much farther north live the Mongols, in a land of wide prairies called steppes. The Dai people live in tropical Yunnan, bordering Vietnam. The life-styles, religions, and customs of the minorities are rich, varied, and usually very old.


## THE GEOGRAPHY OF CHINA

China is one of the world's largest nations, slightly greater in area than the United States. (Only the USSR and Canada are bigger.) Almost every kind of geography can be found in China: steppes, deserts, mountains, tropical lowlands,

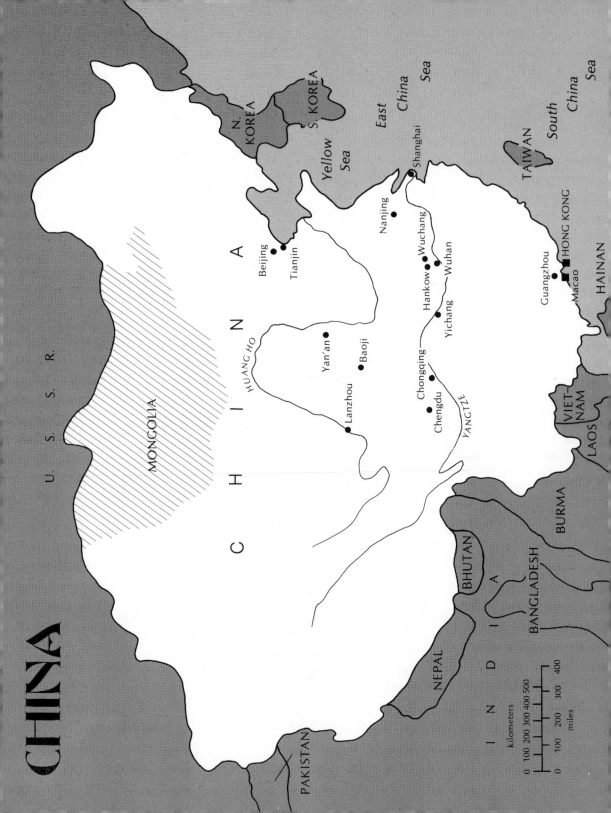

pine forests, and flood-washed river valleys. In all, about two-thirds of China is either mountainous or desert.

Because of China's great geographical differences, many types of climate are found in the country. The south is very wet and hot much of the year. North of the Yangtze River, summers are milder and winters are dry and cold. In Tibet and Mongolia, temperatures plunge far below zero in winter. In the great western deserts, summer temperatures well over 100°F (38°C) are common.

Most of the Chinese people live in the eastern part of the country; nearly 90 percent live on 15 percent of the land. Half of China is sparsely settled, with only 4 percent of the population. Eastern China has some of the world's largest cities, including the capital Beijing (old name: Peking), Shanghai (probably the world's largest city), Tianjin, and Guangzhou [guan-jo] (old name: Canton).


## A LAND OF MIGHTY RIVERS

China's many great rivers have played a major part in Chinese history. The Yangtze (also called the Ch'ang Chiang) is 3,950 miles (6,360 km) long—the third-longest river in the world after the Nile and the Amazon. The Yangtze divides southern from central China, and it runs through some of the most heavily populated areas on earth. Three hundred million people live in the area drained by the mighty river.

Thousands of boats and ships use the Yangtze every day. Tiny sampans rowed by two or three people leave shore for the rich mid-river fishing. Sail-powered junks move animals and grain up- and downriver. Barges piled high with coal maneuver through tricky bends and rapids. Ferries carrying hundreds of people—and goods of every description—fight upriver against the current. Near the

coast the river is thirty miles (48 km) wide. Large oceangoing tankers and freighters carrying cargoes from all over the world follow the river to the great port at Shanghai.

Another great river divides central from northern China. The Yellow River (Huang Ho [pronounced hwang ho]) was known for generations as "the river of sorrows." It has flooded 1,500 times in recorded history, killing hundreds of thousands and driving millions from their homes. Yet the river is a blessing to the people, too. Every year its waters carry millions of tons of silt down from the highlands. The silt turns the water a deep yellow, giving the river its name. The river deposits the silt as a rich layer of soil on the floodplains, producing excellent farmland.

China's many rivers empty into the Pacific Ocean. China has a 4,000-mile (6,440-km) coastline, and the Chinese have long used their coastal waters to fish and trade. Many of the Hakka minority live on colorful fishing boats and go ashore infrequently.

## TRANSPORTATION

Canals connect many of China's rivers. The longest canal in the world was built by the Chinese over a 2,000-year period beginning in the sixth century B.C. The Grand Canal system is about 1,900 miles (3,095 km) long and much of it is still used today.

Many miles of roads and railroads have been built in recent years, but China's transportation system is still far

*Top: a sampan on the Yangtze*
*Bottom: a Yangtze river town*

from modern. Most of China's roads are narrow and un-paved, and there are no true superhighways. The railroad system is only one-ninth the size of the United States', but mile for mile it is probably the most heavily used in the world. Some lines cross extremely rugged country. Over 130 miles (209 km) of the 416-mile (670-km) line from Baoji [bao-gi] to Chengdu [chen-du] had to be tunneled through solid rock.

## NATURAL RESOURCES

China has a shortage of good farmland. Only about one-tenth of the country is well suited to farming. Land that would be rejected as completely unsuitable in many coun-tries is farmed with great care and skill by China's farmers, generally known as peasants. In many areas they have cut ledges called terraces into steep hillsides to gain a few more precious yards of soil for crops. Their hard work has placed China among the world's leaders in the production of rice, wheat, soybeans, tobacco, tea, and cotton.

China is blessed with vast natural resources for energy and industry. Today the country ranks among the world's leaders in coal production. Minerals such as iron ore, urani-um, tungsten, and tin are found in abundance. Vast off-shore oil fields are being developed. Many of China's rivers are being harnessed to provide huge amounts of hydro-electricity.

Despite its great size, its wealth of natural resources, and its incredible pool of human labor and talent, China still lags far behind the United States and most Western na-tions in industrial development and living standards. Why? To find some of the answers, we must turn to China's rich, long, and often sad history.

# 2

## A GLORIOUS
## BUT TROUBLED
## PAST

The great dam near Yichang is only one of many huge projects that Chinese muscle and ingenuity have built in the last 3,000 years. The most famous is the Great Wall, the largest construction project in history. Forty feet (12 m) high in places and wide enough for five horses to gallop abreast, it runs for 1,500 miles (2,400 km) along the northern border of China. Counting bends, dips, and branching walls, its total length exceeds 3,700 miles (5,960 km).

The wall was constructed by the emperor Shih Huangdi [shi hwang-di] (259–209 B.C.). A brilliant but cruel ruler, he founded the Qin [chin] dynasty in 221 B.C. (A dynasty is a ruling family in which power is handed down from one generation to the next, usually from father to eldest son.) The Qin dynasty destroyed most of the power of regional rulers and established the first system of strong central government in China.

Like emperors before him, Shih Huangdi feared the fierce wandering tribes to the north. He decided to con-

struct a barrier against their raids on his settled peaceable subjects. He connected a series of older walls to form a huge new wall. Chinese tradition says that it took thirty years and cost "a life for every stone." So immense was the suffering involved that not long after the emperor died, the people rose and overthrew the dynasty.

Although the Qin dynasty lasted less than twenty years, it changed China forever. All the dynasties that followed would try to establish strong central governments.

The Great Wall was completed by the next dynasty, the Han, and it was repaired and rebuilt by the emperors who ruled in the next 2,000 years. It was not a perfect barrier, but it became a symbol of China's determination to keep the outside world at a distance. The Chinese considered their country and civilization the most advanced in the world. For them, China was the Middle Kingdom, a land located at the center of the world and surrounded by the lands of crude uncivilized people they called barbarians.

## GREAT ACCOMPLISHMENTS

The ancient Chinese had many reasons to consider their civilization the greatest in the world. They knew how to make cast iron 1,500 years before the Europeans did. They invented papermaking, gunpowder, silk weaving, the magnetic compass, and the printing press. China's scientists made major discoveries in mathematics, astronomy, zoolo-

*The Great Wall*

gy, and many other sciences. China's artists painted pictures of wondrous beauty. Its writers composed superb novels and poems. All kinds of crafts were practiced with extraordinary skill. Nowhere were there larger public works, greater cities, or more glorious palaces.

## CONFUCIANISM: AN ANCIENT MORAL CODE

Twenty-five hundred years ago, a minor government official named Confucius became deeply unhappy about the suffering and disorder he saw in Chinese society. He thought long and hard about China's problems and developed a plan for a better society.

In his plan everyone would know his or her place in society and understand his or her relationship with those on levels above and below. Confucius taught that there were five relationships a person had to understand: between husband and wife, parent and child, older and younger brother, friend and friend, and ruler and subject. Confucius suggested strict rules of address and respect to make these relationships work smoothly. The first rule was very similar to the Golden Rule taught by Christ. Confucius said, "Do not do to others what you would not want them to do to you."

Confucius saw few of his ideas accepted in his own time, but other scholars kept them alive. Over 300 years later the Han dynasty adopted the ideas of Confucius. From that distant time until only a few decades ago, Confucianism served as the social and governmental philosophy of China.

Although the principles of Confucianism were good, they were not always put to good use. The ruling classes used them to justify their oppression of the lower classes. Women were placed in a position of lifelong inferiority. Scholars were frequently so busy studying the Confucian classics that they didn't have time to study other thinkers or to do original work of their own.

Eventually Chinese society became so rigid that it was very difficult to introduce new ideas. The Middle Kingdom paid heavily for this shortcoming.

# DYNASTIES
# AND MANDARINS

The Chinese believed a dynasty ruled with the approval of the gods—with the "mandate of heaven." If a dynasty ruled well, it might remain in power for hundreds of years. If it ruled poorly, the mandate of heaven would be "withdrawn" and the dynasty overthrown.

Below the emperor and his immediate family was a remarkable class of highly educated public officials, the mandarins, who carried out the day-to-day administration of the vast Middle Kingdom. Unlike any other ruling class in the world, the mandarins held their positions not because of blood ties to the royal family but because of their intelligence and education. Although dynasties rose and fell, the mandarins maintained their power for more than 2,000 years.

A mandarin's education was based on the writings of the wise man Confucius (551?–479? B.C.). His teachings provided a code of behavior for Chinese society. Everyone from the emperor to the poorest peasant had duties to fulfill. If all acted correctly, there would be peace and harmony. By studying the teachings of Confucius, those who hoped to become mandarins were supposed to learn the principles of fair and efficient government.

In theory, under this system a young man from the lowest class could rise to the highest levels in government if he had the brains and energy to master the knowledge needed to pass the government examinations. Some succeeded, but the expense of getting the proper education kept most young men—no matter how bright—out of the mandarin class.

Below the governing classes lived the vast majority of Chinese. Some were craftsmen or merchants. Others were monks, fishermen, or soldiers. Nine out of ten were poor peasant-farmers, and their lives were the hardest. They worked long hours in all seasons, forever at the mercy of the weather, bandits, and the rich landlords who owned most of the land. While the small ruling classes lived in luxury, most Chinese were very poor; when crops failed, millions starved.

For over 2,000 years, Chinese society remained much the same. Dynasties came and went every few hundred years. There were civil wars and wars against foreign invaders. Famines, floods, and diseases killed millions. Corruption was commonplace among the mandarins and the landlords. Despite everything, the Middle Kingdom endured from generation to generation, and everyday life was usually peaceful.

While China sought to preserve tradition and harmony, the nations of the West pursued change and progress. The inevitable collision would destroy the old way of life in China.

# 3

## A COLLISION OF CULTURES

For many centuries the emperors tried to keep the Middle Kingdom isolated from the outside world. But not even the Great Wall and China's natural barriers could protect the Middle Kingdom forever.

By the mid-1600s, many ships from the West were visiting China. The emperors became nervous about the influence of the Westerners, particularly the Christian missionaries who followed the traders. In 1757 the reigning "son of heaven" confined all foreign traders to the city of Guangzhou. This displeased the Western nations, but the Chinese government refused to give in to their demands for freer trade. Eventually one of the most unjust wars in modern history changed this situation.

### THE OPIUM WAR

Many Chinese were addicted to opium, a powerful narcotic drug. For a few cents a man could smoke a pipe of opium and forget the backbreaking labor of his days. But the drug left the addict depressed, without energy, and all too willing to spend his last few pennies on another pipe.

British traders were making large profits from the importation of opium. The Chinese government tried to stamp out the trade, but it continued. When government troops seized and burned a large shipment of opium in Guangzhou in 1839, the British declared war. The Chinese troops with their ancient weapons were no match for the well-trained and -armed Europeans. In 1842 the emperor asked for peace. The peace treaty opened five ports to foreign trade and gave the British the port of Hong Kong.

## BLOODY REBELLIONS

The Qing [ching] dynasty was already unpopular with many Chinese. (The Qing emperors were not Han, but Manchus, members of a northern tribe that had breached the Great Wall and established their dynasty in 1644.) After the Opium War many Chinese felt the mandate of heaven had been withdrawn. In 1850 a huge rebellion broke out in southeastern China.

The Taiping Rebellion lasted fourteen years and cost up to twenty million lives. The Taipings wanted not only a new dynasty but many reforms in Chinese society, including land reform and equal rights for women. Several Western powers decided they preferred to do business with the weak Qing dynasty. They supplied military aid and advisers to the Manchus, and the rebellion was put down.

## A TOTTERING DYNASTY

The next half century was very sad for China. Too corrupt and weak to govern effectively, the dynasty tottered. The

European powers, soon joined by Japan, divided China into "spheres of influence"—areas where they, not the Chinese government, ruled in all but name.

The United States did not carve out such a sphere of influence, but it called for an Open Door policy giving all nations equal trading rights in China. (No one bothered to ask the Chinese if they wanted to deal with the West at all!) This policy, accepted without enthusiasm by the other powers, was soon and repeatedly violated.

In the countryside the people seethed with discontent. There was poverty, hunger, and banditry. Rich landlords owned more than half the land, and farmers were forced to work it at near-starvation wages. Other old and terrible customs continued as well. Even minor criminals were executed or maimed for life. The young daughters of wealthy families had their feet tightly bound with cloth, leaving them in adulthood with deformed feet and a shuffling, dainty step that was thought to be beautiful. Poor people often exposed unwanted children (particularly girls) to the elements to die. Some Christian missionaries did what they could to bring a better life to the poor, but most Westerners in China were only interested in ways of making money.

In addition, the Chinese ruling classes had become almost unbelievably corrupt. The ruler during this period was the Empress Dowager Cixi [tsu-shi] (1835–1908). When her infant son became emperor in 1861, she became regent—a caretaker appointed to govern until her child was old enough to rule. However, after her son died in 1875, she appointed her young nephew, Kuang Hsu [kwang su] (1871–1908), emperor and continued to rule according to her often bizarre whims. (For example, she built a huge marble boat on the lake at the summer palace outside Bei-

[17]

*The famous marble boat at the summer palace. A symbol of imperial decadence, it was built with naval funds.*

jing with funds intended for the modernization of the Chinese navy.)

## A BRIEF ATTEMPT
## AT REFORM

Many educated Chinese knew that the nation had to change. Some had studied in the United States or Europe and were aware of the power of Western technology and industry. In 1898 the reformers convinced the young emperor that China must modernize or be divided by the greedy Westerners. For a hundred days, a stream of reform orders came from the throne. The old civil service exams based on the Confucian classics would be changed. New schools, teaching both Chinese and Western subjects, would be set up. People with modern skills would be promoted. The army and navy would be modernized. Corruption would be stamped out. The laws of the nation would be reformed.

The empress dowager did not approve and stepped in. Kuang Hsu was imprisoned on an island in the lake at the summer palace. Many of his advisers were executed. His decrees were withdrawn. The dynasty returned to its corrupt and backward-looking ways.

## THE BOXER REBELLION

In 1900 thousands rose in revolt. Being ruled by the Manchus was bad enough, but being ruled by Western "white devils" could not be tolerated. The Society of Righteous and Harmonious Fists, or Boxers as they were called by Westerners, would throw out the foreigners and restore the Middle Kingdom to its glory. The Boxers killed missionaries and traders by the hundreds and then marched on Beijing.

With support from the dynasty, the Boxers laid siege to the area of the city occupied by the Western embassies. The troops and civilians inside held out for eight weeks and were finally rescued by Western troops marching inland from the coast. The revenge of the Western powers was terrible. Thousands of Boxers and even people suspected of sympathizing with them were hunted down and executed without trial. Western troops and civilians, even missionaries, looted everything they could find of value. The government of China was fined $333 million for its part in the uprising.

## REFORM COMES TOO LATE

Allowed to keep her power, Cixi reluctantly ordered many of the reforms that Kuang Hsu had attempted. Both the emperor and his aunt died in the same month of 1908. (Some say she ordered his murder.) However, one of Cixi's last acts was to promise the Chinese people a constitutional monarchy, in which the emperor would be a figurehead and the real power would rest with the people. But it was too late. Not even massive reform could save the system that had ruled China since the Qin dynasty over 2,000 years before. What would replace it? It would take more decades of turmoil and the spilled blood of millions to find the answer.

# 4

## YEARS OF
## TURMOIL

The fall of the last dynasty came with remarkable speed and little bloodshed by the standards of Chinese history. In September 1911, troops in the city of Wuchang [wu-chan] in east central China mutinied. The garrison commander joined the mutineers, and the revolution spread quickly. By the end of the year, nearly all of China's provincial governors were calling for the overthrow of the Manchus. The head of the imperial army, Yuan Shikai (1859–1916), fought the rebels briefly and then went over to their side. The last mandate of heaven had been withdrawn. The child-emperor quit the throne in early January 1912, and Dr. Sun Yat-sen [sun yat-shan] (1866–1925) was sworn in as first president of the new Republic of China.

Dr. Sun had worked many years for this day. Since 1895 he had been organizing groups to overthrow the dynasty. Forced to leave China, he had traveled widely, seeking support from Chinese living abroad. He had developed a program for a new China based on three principles—nationalism (the people should strive to build a strong China

capable of managing its affairs without the interference of other nations); democracy (government by the people through elected representatives); and "the people's livelihood" (the wealth of China should be managed for the good of all).

Less than two months later, Dr. Sun resigned the presidency in favor of Yuan Shikai. Dr. Sun hoped that Yuan, with his greater military power, could reunite the country. However, Yuan was not dedicated to democratic revolution. Soon it became obvious that he intended to found a dynasty of his own. The revolution had been betrayed.

## JAPAN'S GREED GROWS

In 1914, Europe was torn apart by World War I. While the Western powers concentrated all their efforts on the war, Japan moved to expand its influence in China. Japan took over Germany's sphere of influence in China and delivered the "Twenty-one Demands" to Yuan. The Japanese wanted more special privileges, including the right to oversee the workings of the Chinese government and police force. Yuan needed Japanese money to establish his new dynasty, but Japan was demanding too much in return. Although Yuan sought the support of the Western powers in refusing some of the Japanese conditions, he eventually had to agree to most of them.

Yuan died in 1916, his dreams of a new dynasty in tatters. The central government in Beijing became a shaky coalition of military leaders called warlords. Each warlord

*Dr. Sun Yat-sen*

[23]

ruled in his own region and frequently fought his rivals. The common people suffered greatly.

Dr. Sun had not given up his dream of a democratic revolution. He reorganized and strengthened his party, now called the Guomindang. The Guomindang would soon have a rival for the future of revolution in China.

### COMMUNISM

The basic idea of communism is very old: private property is evil. Throughout history, many thinkers and groups have believed that greed for money and possessions always creates a society of "haves and have nots." A better society could be built if all property were held in common and everyone were provided with the necessities of life according to his or her needs.

The founder of modern communism was the German thinker Karl Marx (1818–83). Marx believed that all history could be explained as a conflict between the ruling classes who owned the means of production (factories, for example) and the working classes who provided the muscle but received too small a share of the profits. Marx felt that eventually the world's workers would rebel and establish common ownership of the means of production. The new society would be classless, with all resources managed for the common good.

V.I. Lenin (1870–1924), a Russian revolutionary, developed Marx's ideas and led a successful communist revolution in Russia in 1917. However, The Union of Soviet Socialist Republics (USSR) did not develop into an ideal communist society. Joseph Stalin (1879–1953) ruled the USSR as a dictator after Lenin's death. The people had few personal liberties and many were killed or put in labor camps.

Mao Zedong and Zhou Enlai, the leaders of the Chinese Communist Party, believed China could develop an ideal communist society. But they were also violent revolutionaries who knew bloodshed would be necessary to sweep away the old system.

## THE CHINESE
## COMMUNIST PARTY

A few young revolutionaries were becoming converts to communism. They saw the 1917 Communist revolution in Russia as a model for revolution in China. The newly named Union of Soviet Socialist Republics (USSR) had won many Chinese friends by announcing that Russia would give up its sphere of influence in China. In 1921, with the aid of Soviet Union advisers, the Chinese Communist Party was founded.

Dr. Sun distrusted many aspects of communism. He felt his revolutionary philosophy was more appropriate for China. He agreed to allow individual Communists into the Guomindang, but insisted that the Chinese Communist Party disband. Under pressure from their Soviet advisers, the Communists agreed, but continued to expand the party in secret. The Guomindang started accepting Soviet aid and advice.

## CHIANG KAISHEK
## TAKES POWER

The Guomindang established a revolutionary government in Guangzhou in 1923. Dr. Sun Yat-sen died in 1925 and was succeeded by his chief military adviser, Chiang Kaishek [jiang kai-shek] (1887–1975). In 1926 Chiang led the armies of the new government north to fight the warlords. As his troops advanced, Communist members of the Guomindang organized strikes in many large cities. The local governments were often at the point of collapse when Chiang's troops arrived.

With the secret help of the Soviet advisers, the Communists were also proving skillful at gaining power in the Guomindang revolutionary government, now located in Wuhan. Chiang, who represented the more conservative wing of the Guomindang, was disturbed by the growing power of the Communists. He was in favor of Dr. Sun's principle of nationalism, but direct rule by the people threatened too many of his powerful and wealthy friends. Somehow he had to stop the Communists from gaining control of the revolution.

Early in the spring of 1927, Chiang's troops surrounded Shanghai, China's largest city. A young Communist named Zhou Enlai [jo en-lai] had already led an uprising and established a Communist government in the city. Chiang was furious; the Communists were out of control. He sent a message to the Wuhan government demanding that it move to Nanjing where it would be reorganized as a conservative government under his direction. The government refused. Chiang's troops entered Shanghai and slaughtered the Communists by the thousands. Within days the Communist Party was reeling under a massive assault all over southern China. Those who could escape went into hiding.

Chiang set up a new government in Nanjing and prepared to march on Wuhan. The Wuhan government gave in to Chiang's demands and disbanded. The Soviet advisers were sent home. Chiang and his government ruled southern China.

In 1928 Chiang defeated or won over the last of the warlords and completed his march to Beijing. It was a hol-

*The young Chiang Kaishek*

low victory in many ways. The Guomindang was now a conservative party very unlike what Dr. Sun had hoped to build. For many people it seemed that the promises of the Nationalist revolution had come to very little. Chiang ruled as a dictator. His government was corrupt, and poverty and hardship were as widespread as ever. New warlords controlled half the country, sometimes collecting taxes fifty years in advance. Landlords bought up more land, making the life of the peasants even harder. In 1928–30 famine killed five million, and four hundred thousand peasants sold themselves into servitude. The government did nothing.

## THE COMMUNISTS
## REBUILD

In the mountains of Jiangxi [jiang-shi] Province in southern China, the Communists were rebuilding their party. They were led by two of the most remarkable men of this century, Mao Zedong (1893–1976) and Zhou Enlai (1898–1976). Mao was the elder son of a fairly well-off landowner. He had received both a classical and a modern education as a young man. Zhou was the son of a prominent mandarin family, spoke several languages, and was a master negotiator. Both had shown great ability as Communist organizers. Together they would change Chinese history.

Their plan was to convert the peasants to their cause. After centuries of poverty and the terrible disappointment of the Nationalist revolution, the peasants were ready for communism. The Communist leaders made strict rules for their political organizers and troops: There would be no looting, no raping, no abuse of the peasants. Troops would pay for what they ate. All would treat the peasants with respect.

## CHIANG PREPARES
## TO STRIKE

Chiang realized that his purge had missed not only Mao and Zhou, but many others of great intelligence and ability. If he did not destroy the Communists quickly, they would soon be a major problem again. That possibility was much on his mind when Japan invaded Manchuria in 1931, quickly capturing the vast province and much of China's modern industry.

Instead of fighting the Japanese, Chiang chose to attack the Communists. For several years the Japanese continued to take chunks of Chinese territory without great opposition, while Chiang mounted campaigns against the Communist "bandits."

By 1934 the pressure on the Communists had grown so great that desperate action was necessary. The Communist Red Army broke through the ring of surrounding Nationalist armies and retreated to the west. The Long March was one of the most incredible military feats in history. Mao and his forces crossed high mountains and raging rivers, fought hundreds of battles and skirmishes, and endured hunger, cold, and rain. Finally, after 6,000 miles (9,660 km) and twelve months of almost constant movement, they set up their new headquarters at Yan'an in remote Shaanxi Province. Some 80,000 of the original 100,000 marchers had died on the journey, but the Red Army had survived and made millions of converts to communism.


## JAPAN INVADES

In 1937 the Japanese staged an all-out invasion of China. Chiang's generals forced him to make peace with the Com-

munists so that Nationalists and Communists could unite in China's defense. But the Japanese troops were far better armed and trained than the Chinese. Chiang was driven from his capital at Nanjing, then from Hankow, before finally establishing a third capital at remote Chongqing [chon-jing], far up the Yangtze. The Japanese invaders were brutal. In the "Rape of Nanjing" alone, they killed 150,000 Chinese.

However, the immensity of China eventually slowed the invaders. Chiang held out and began to receive military aid from the United States. But rather than go on the offensive against the Japanese, Chiang hoarded his new equipment. Even while the Japanese held most of eastern China, Chiang spent much of his time planning a renewed campaign against the Communists.

World War II ended in 1945 when the United States dropped two atomic bombs on Japan. Within hours of the Japanese surrender, civil war was raging in China. Although the Nationalists had superiority in numbers and weapons, they were doomed. Corruption and cowardice had lost Chiang's government the support of the majority of Chinese. Mao's forces were battle-hardened and committed; this time the revolution would succeed. The war dragged on for four bloody years. In 1949 Chiang, finally forced to admit defeat, retreated to the island of Taiwan. On the mainland, the victorious Communists declared the People's Republic of China.

*A painting of Mao Zedong
on the Long March*

# 5

## THE MAKING OF THE PEOPLE'S REPUBLIC

Huge problems faced the new leaders of China in 1949. For over a century, there had rarely been peace in China. The nation had little modern industry. There was terrible poverty in most parts of the country. Much of the outside world was hostile.

As chairman of the Communist Party, Mao was the most powerful leader in China. He began a series of sweeping reforms. The land of the rich landlords was confiscated and given to the peasants. Businesses and factories were taken over by the government. Food and other goods were rationed. Prices were fixed. Grain was stockpiled in case of famine. Education and medical care were improved and made available to more people.

## A CONTINUING REVOLUTION

"Revolution," Mao had written, "is not a dinner party," and many people died in these early years. "Reactionaries" —people who had belonged to the ruling classes or had opposed the revolution—were rooted out. Hundreds of thousands, perhaps millions, were tried by "people's courts" in mass meetings of angry peasants and then executed. Others were sent to labor camps to be "reeducated." The class system that had existed for many centuries was destroyed very quickly.

Mao believed that the institutions of old China must also be destroyed. Confucianism, the philosophy that had justified the old system, was denounced. Communism and the "thought of Mao Zedong" were put in its place. Churches and temples were closed or put under tight government control. For the revolution to succeed, "constant vigilance" was necessary. The party must destroy all tendencies of the people to slip back into their old ways —whatever the damage to individual freedoms.

The Communist party ruled in place of the old system. Many party members were people of ability and dedication, but others held their positions mainly because of their loyalty to the party. War, purges, and the Nationalists' flight to Taiwan had robbed China of many of its best-educated and most talented people. The task of rebuilding China would be difficult.

## THE KOREAN WAR AND A HOSTILE WORLD

The Communist leaders had many reasons to fear for the future of the revolution. Most of the Western nations had deep misgivings about the new system in China. The United States was particularly hostile, continuing to support and arm the Nationalist government of Taiwan. Chiang swore he would return and retake the mainland.

In 1950 civil war broke out in Korea between the Communist North and the republican South. The United Nations approved a "police action" in support of the South, and soon the UN forces were winning the war. The Chinese threw their troops into the conflict late in 1950. The war lasted three years and soured relations between China and the United States for many years.

## GOVERNING THE PEOPLE'S REPUBLIC

The Communists established a republican form of government in 1949. In theory all people would have a say in how the People's Republic was governed, but the reality is very different.

According to the constitution, the supreme governing body is the National People's Congress. It is elected by congresses in China's thirty provinces, autonomous regions (large, sparsely inhabited areas with a high minority population), and municipalities (very large cities). There are also congresses at a lower level, directly elected by the people. The National People's Congress meets in the Great Hall of the People in Beijing, passing laws that are carried out by the State Council and the agencies under its control.

In reality the National People's Congress has very little power. It only rubber-stamps the decisions of the Communist Party; the party has the real power in China. The party is organized much like the national government, with regional congresses and a national congress. There are about forty million party members. An energetic party member can rise through the ranks, but the top levels are still controlled by aging veterans of the war with the Nationalists. The highest level of the party is the Politburo. All the major decisions for governing China are made by its twenty-seven members.

The higher levels of the government and the party overlap. A high official in the party usually holds an equally high position in the government. At lower levels, some nonparty members may hold positions, but only with the confidence of the party. For all practical purposes, the party is the government.

# THE ELDER BROTHERS

About the only nation the Chinese thought they could depend on was the USSR. In the early 1950s the Chinese leaders urged the people to learn from their "elder brothers"—the thousands of advisers sent by the Soviet Union. The Chinese copied the Soviet Union's governmental, educational, military, and police systems. Following the Soviet example, the central government issued "five-year plans" for modernizing the economy. Few decisions were left to the workers or peasants.

By 1956 Mao had begun to doubt much of the Soviet advice. Progress wasn't coming about fast enough. He decided to confiscate the private land of the peasants and organize collective farms where huge tracts of land would be worked by armies of peasants. In theory, more land could be efficiently cultivated in this way. But there was a flaw in the theory—without control of their own land and the crops it produced, the farmers lost much of their enthusiasm for hard work. The Soviet advisers, who had seen the dismal failure of collective farms in the USSR, objected. To the disappointment of the peasants and the dismay of the Soviet advisers, Mao persisted. Agricultural production fell.

Faced with another failure, Mao decided to rally the people to the cause of modernization. If the Chinese people were given more chance to express their ideas, they might work harder. Mao declared the Hundred Flowers Campaign with the words: "Let a hundred flowers bloom and a hundred thoughts contend."

Mao wasn't prepared for what happened. The pent-up anger of many people, particularly the educated intellectuals, produced harsh criticism of the party, the government's policies, and even communism itself. Mao abruptly ended the campaign, calling the critics "poisonous weeds." Tens of thousands of intellectuals were arrested and sent to prisons or labor camps—some for as long as twenty years. Once again China had lost many of its best-educated and most talented people.

## THE GREAT LEAP FORWARD

What was Mao to do now? Others might have turned to more conservative policies, but that was not in Mao's nature. Ignoring the protests of his Soviet advisers, he ordered the most radical plan yet—the Great Leap Forward.

The plan called for a complete reorganization of Chinese society. China's vast population would be divided into tens of thousands of "communes." Almost all aspects of individual and family life would be directed by the commune authorities. Party officials called cadres would control the housing, education, medical care, work assignments, recreation, and political expression of all commune members. Working together unselfishly, China's peasants would modernize China overnight.

The communes were ordered to vastly increase agricultural and industrial production. The wisdom and enthusiasm of the people and the thought of Mao Zedong would make all things possible. But the Great Leap Forward soon turned into a giant step backward. Cadres who knew nothing about farming directed the planting of rice and the

*Top: the exterior of commune living quarters*
*Bottom: a commune woman making brooms*

[36]

crops failed. When a great increase in steel production was ordered, unskilled cadres directed equally unskilled peasants in building thousands of crude blast furnaces. Every available ounce of scrap metal was gathered—some families even contributed their pots and pans. The steel produced was of such terrible quality that it was unusable.

Dozens of such efforts produced similarly shoddy results. Energy and resources that China could not spare were wasted at a spectacular rate. Forests were cut down, the wood burned as fuel or poorly used. Soil erosion ruined farmland. Agricultural production plunged. The weather turned bad and the age-old curse of Chinese life struck: famine. In the terrible year of 1960, an estimated twenty million people starved. The Great Leap Forward ended in disaster.

Disgusted with Mao, the USSR became openly hostile and withdrew its advisers. Each country denounced the other for "deviating" from true communism. The Communist giants had become enemies.

## MAO'S POWER EBBS

Practical members of the party now began to argue against Mao's faith in the common people's ability to modernize China. They said that China had to train a new class of scientists and technicians. Among these "pragmatists" were Premier Zhou Enlai, the chief of foreign policy; Liu Shaoqi [li-u shao-chi], the president of the republic; and Deng Xiaoping [deng shiao-ping], one of his main deputies.

Although Mao still held supreme power as chairman of the Communist party, for a time the pragmatists gained influence. China rebounded from the disaster of the Great

Leap Forward. By the mid-1960s more skilled direction of the economy had raised the Chinese standard of living to its highest level in history.

## THE CULTURAL REVOLUTION

Mao felt that his power was slipping away. In addition he believed that China was losing sight of the goals of the revolution. Party cadres, intellectuals, and technicians were taking the place of the ruling classes of old China. The ideal of a classless society was being lost.

In 1966 Mao took a desperate measure and declared the Great Cultural Revolution. He enlisted millions of young people in an army to overthrow the new ruling classes. He instructed them to "turn the guns on the headquarters." The Red Guards carried out their orders with a vengeance. Hundreds of thousands of intellectuals and government officials were accused of deviating from the thought of Mao Zedong. They were beaten, publicly humiliated and imprisoned or sent to work in distant communes. Artists, scientists, college professors, doctors, and countless other well-educated people were soon cleaning latrines, slopping hogs, and planting rice.

Liu Shaoqi died under house arrest on an isolated commune. Deng Xiaoping was sent into rural exile. Only Zhou was able to keep his position. The excesses of the Red Guards continued for several years, during which they persecuted perhaps a hundred million people. Children denounced their parents as "capitalist roaders." Red Guards broke into homes in search of anything that could be considered "counterrevolutionary." Any movie, play, book, or painting that did not glorify the wisdom of Mao was condemned. Priceless art and magnificent buildings dating from the old China were destroyed. Pitched battles were fought in the streets between Red Guards and workers tired of their bullying. Most of the world thought China had gone mad.

Through it all Zhou was heroic. Unable to put an end to the chaos decreed by Mao, he worked hard to tame the movement. His intervention may have saved China from another civil war. Finally, however, the Red Guards turned on him, too. A mob marched to Mao's residence to denounce Zhou as yet another counterrevolutionary. But Mao lost his temper. Zhou, his old comrade-in-arms, had helped found the party, survived Chiang's purges, endured the horrors of the Long March, fought for almost a quarter of a century against the Japanese and the Guomindang, and finally stood at Mao's side when the People's Republic of China was born. A counterrevolutionary? No! Zhou was the model revolutionary! Mao angrily told the Red Guards to go home.

That night marked the beginning of the end for the Red Guards and the Cultural Revolution. It also marked the beginning of a new phase in Chinese politics. Several more years of turmoil would follow, but the era of violent revolution was drawing to a close.

# 6

## NEW LEADERS, NEW HOPE

In 1969 the army crushed the power of the Red Guards. The worst of the Cultural Revolution was over, but the turmoil faded slowly. Gradually the pragmatists were readmitted to the high ranks of the party. Regaining their former positions was not easy. Mao was an old man by now, increasingly under the influence of his wife, Jiang Qing, [jiang ching], a radical who wanted to continue the Cultural Revolution.

Zhou, too, had grown old. In his last years he hoped to end China's long isolation from much of the rest of the world. He met in secret with Henry Kissinger, national security adviser to the president of the United States. Together they planned a dramatic event. In early 1972, to the astonishment of the world, President Richard M. Nixon flew to China. A lifelong anticommunist, Nixon had a friendly meeting with Mao and was soon toasting Zhou at a banquet in Beijing's Great Hall of the People. A great wall of distrust had been breached.

# THE DEATH OF THE
# REVOLUTIONARY LEADERS

Mao and Zhou died in 1976. There was a great outpouring of grief when the news of Zhou's death was announced. The people had come to view this quiet and wise man as the "elder brother" of all Chinese. Even in the worst of times, he had been there to preserve the country and the revolution. The death of Mao was mourned with fewer tears. "The great helmsman" had become more an object of awe and fear than of love.

Without Mao's protection, Jiang Qing and her fellow radicals quickly lost power to the pragmatists. Jiang Qing and three other top leaders were arrested. Labeled the Gang of Four, they were convicted of treason and sent to prison. At last the pragmatists, led by Deng Xiaoping, ruled China.

They faced great problems. The economy had been badly hurt by the ten-year Cultural Revolution. The government was inefficient, and the educational system was a disaster. Much needed to be done to put China back on the path to modernization. Deng had a plan that would bring a very different kind of revolution to China.

## DENG XIAOPING

Deng Xiaoping is a tiny, smiling man, his face almost child-like at times. Yet his physical appearance cannot hide his intelligence and iron will. He has been a revolutionary all his long life. A veteran of the Long March, he held positions of great power in the party until his disgrace during the Cultural Revolution.

During his long years in rural exile, Deng reached some

conclusions about Mao's brand of communism. One of the most important was that China must avoid another "cult of personality" like the one that had grown up around Mao. With the pragmatists in power, Deng took a modest position as vice chairman of the party and had younger men elected to the top offices in the party and the government. Deng would exert his influence through others.

Deng also realized that although Mao was dead, the thought of Mao Zedong still had tremendous power. Carefully he set about cutting Mao's reputation down to size. It was explained that Mao had fallen out of touch with the people in his old age and made errors under the influence of the Gang of Four. Although China would be forever grateful to Mao for his contributions to the revolution, it was time to move on. The many pictures of the "the great helmsman" quietly disappeared from China's buildings.

## THE FOUR MODERNIZATIONS

Instead of the thought of Mao Zedong, Deng and the other pragmatists emphasized the Four Modernizations. All Chinese were to support a great effort to modernize the military, science and technology, agriculture, and industry.

The Chinese army was the largest in the world, but it was poorly armed and trained. New weapons would be provided. The army would train hard and adopt tactics more suitable to modern warfare. It would help construct large public works projects for the modernization of China.

Before the Cultural Revolution, Chinese scientists had been making great strides in mastering the science and technology of the West. China had exploded nuclear bombs and launched earth satellites. Now many scientists were recalled from rural exile and the laboratories were re-opened. China's schools set about training a new generation of scientists and technicians.

During the Cultural Revolution, schools and universities had often closed while students went to the countryside to "learn from the peasants." When the schools were open, students usually received a poor education. Most of the skilled teachers—hated intellectuals—were in rural exile, their places taken by incompetents more interested in teaching the thought of Mao Zedong than practical knowledge. Almost an entire generation of young people had lost the chance for a meaningful education.

The pragmatists now recalled most of the disgraced teachers from the countryside, and schools opened full-time. No longer was the thought of Mao Zedong the most important subject. Students were taught practical skills that would help China modernize. Thousands of the best students were sent to foreign countries to study.

Although these changes were great, they seemed small compared to what Deng planned for agriculture and industry.

## MAJOR CHANGES
## IN THE ECONOMY

Deng and the other pragmatists realized that the ideal of communism—everyone working unselfishly for the common good—simply wasn't working. Unless people were given the chance to get ahead, few would work as hard as they could. In the capitalist Western countries, there were too many rich people and too many poor ones. Still, the average standard of living was higher than in China or the

USSR. Most irritating of all, the economy of nationalist Taiwan—"the other China"—was booming. How was the People's Republic to catch up to the capitalist nations and still remain a communist country that met the needs of all? Deng's plan was to set up a "responsibility" system with many avenues open to free enterprise.

### THE OTHER CHINA

When the Communists defeated the Nationalist armies in 1949, Chiang Kaishek retreated to the island of Taiwan (also called Formosa), off the southeastern coast of the mainland. Protected by the friendship of the United States, the Nationalists have ruled the island ever since.

On paper the Republic of China is a democracy. In reality political power has rested with a few. Chiang kept tight control until his death in 1975. His son, Chiang Chingkuo [jiang chin-kwo], is the current president. He has relaxed some of the limits on political expression.

Chiang claimed the Nationalists would someday retake the mainland. In reply Mao threatened to invade Taiwan. Words have been quieter in recent years. The United States now recognizes the Communists as the rightful rulers of the mainland. Although the United States still provides Taiwan with modern weapons, it does not encourage any dreams of invading the mainland. Today the leaders of the People's Republic say they will not invade Taiwan but will find a peaceful method for reuniting China. They have promised to allow Taiwan to keep its free-enterprise economy and even its armed forces. The Taiwanese leaders have shown little interest in political unification and no formal talks have been held. However, trade is growing between the two Chinas.

Deng Xiaoping and the current pragmatic leaders of the People's Republic have studied Taiwan's thriving economy. With only nineteen million people and limited natural resources, Taiwan has become an important manufacturing and trading nation. In the future even more of mainland China's economy may be based on the Taiwanese model.

Many factory work units were told they could fix their own work rules, production goals, and prices in competition with other factories. Profits—unacceptable in Mao's China—would mean higher wages for the workers. Those who showed special ability or effort would be rewarded with bonuses.

In the countryside, peasants no longer had to work in large groups on the commune land. Instead each family or small groups of families could sign contracts with the commune administration to farm a portion of the land. Part of what they produced would be returned to the government. The rest they could sell to whomever they wished at whatever price they could get. Free markets developed and agricultural production soared.

While keeping many of their old functions in housing, education, and medical care, communes became freer places renamed "districts." The cadres lost much of their power to control all aspects of people's lives, and the peasants were now allowed to make most decisions themselves.

In both the cities and the countryside small private enterprises were encouraged. Many businesses sprang up, often run by groups of young people waiting for jobs after finishing school. Restaurants, photography studios, repair shops, and the like were soon doing a thriving trade.

## OPPOSITION REMAINS

Today most people are enthusiastic about the Four Modernizations, particularly the increased free enterprise in the

*Buying chickens and*
*ducks in a free market*

[47]

economy. However, many party cadres, particularly those who gained power during the Cultural Revolution, remain opposed to Deng's quiet revolution.

Deng has taken action to protect his plans. He has streamlined the government, firing many who did little. He has placed pragmatists in positions of power. Recently it was announced that all forty million party members will have to reregister in the near future. It is likely that many who disagree with Deng's pragmatic plans will not be readmitted to the party.

## OTHER REFORMS

The pragmatists are seeking friends outside China. The 1960s propaganda of "exporting revolution" is no longer heard. Tourists now travel in China with few restrictions. Foreign businesspeople are invited to make contracts with the government. China participates in many UN organizations.

Deng has also directed the National People's Congress to write the first complete set of laws for China since the Communist takeover. For thirty years no such detailed code of law existed. During the Cultural Revolution, the Red Guards freely punished people for not following the thought of Mao Zedong. Now the people will have written laws to protect them.

Yet the People's Republic under Deng is far from being a democracy. The Communist Party holds all the power, although it allows the existence of a handful of other parties to give the appearance of political liberty. Freedom of religion is limited. The government controls televison and radio broadcasts, newspapers, and magazines. Free elections are held at the local and factory levels, but not above. Free speech is allowed only up to a point; a too-violent critic of the party or party policy still risks punishment. Many freedoms we take for granted are tightly controlled in China —even the freedom to travel from place to place, to choose one's job, or to have more than one child.

# COURTSHIP, MARRIAGE, AND CHILDREARING

Life has never been easy for the majority of Chinese. Constant hardships gave the ancient Chinese a strong sense of family. Unless a family worked together, it could not survive; many hands were needed to raise a crop. Since medical care was poor—if it existed at all—many children died long before reaching adulthood. A peasant family's security traditionally depended on having many children, especially sons.

Today China has more than a billion people. Further population growth threatens to overwhelm the nation's ability to feed itself. The new, pragmatic leaders of China say that the tradition of large families must end. This is far from the only family tradition that is changing.

## COURTSHIP

In old China most marriages were arranged by parents. The young couple might never have met before the wedding day. The new wife moved in with her husband's family. She brought with her a dowry—money or valuable goods her father had promised her husband's family. She would spend her life performing domestic chores, forever submissive to her husband and the older members of his family. (In wealthy families, she might never leave the family compound again!)

Today women are guaranteed equal rights under the constitution; arranged marriages and dowries are forbidden. No doubt some marriages are still arranged and dowries agreed on, but it is no longer common practice. Many young couples now live away from their parents, but it is just as likely that a family will include one or two aged parents.

In today's China a young person can look openly for a mate. Love has become an acceptable goal. For many, however, the search is difficult. Chinese young people tend to be very modest, and they find meeting people of the opposite sex a trying experience. Most couples are introduced by friends or relatives and spend many months—sometimes years—shyly courting. Affection is rarely displayed in public, and premarital sex is uncommon.

To promote population control, the government has set the minimum age for marriage at twenty-two for men and twenty for women. But even marrying this young is discouraged, and young people are urged instead to work hard for the Four Modernizations and the party. In their late twenties—still unmarried and increasingly anxious —many ambitious workers will go to great lengths to find a mate. Many newspapers publish advertisements from those looking for husbands or wives. The problem has become so acute that the old profession of matchmaking is thriving in

China. Matchmakers offer selections of photographs and descriptions of possible mates; some even use videotapes.

## WEDDING CEREMONIES

A Chinese wedding is usually a simple affair. The couple must appear before a government official to be pronounced husband and wife. Some couples also have a traditional ceremony as well, but the Communist Party does not encourage any religious display. A member of the party risks a black mark on his or her record by having anything to do with religion at any time.

After the civil ceremony, the young couple are likely to meet with one or two dozen friends and family in a crowded room for dinner, music, and perhaps some dancing if space can be found. Lavish wedding parties are frowned on by the party. Only some of the national minorities regularly have elaborate ceremonies and parties.

## SETTING UP HOUSEKEEPING

Newlyweds have many worries ahead. Housing is scarce in China, and they may have to wait months or even years for an apartment or home of their own. Until then, they live with his or her parents. Sometimes, with so little room available, they must live apart.

The couple may also be separated by their work. For example, the wife may be assigned to work on the dam at Yichang, while her husband works in a factory in Wuhan 200 miles (322 km) away. Others may be separated by far greater distances, and it is not uncommon for husbands and wives to see each other only a few weeks a year.

## HAVING CHILDREN

The risk of overpopulation in China is so great that strong measures have been taken. People are expected to ask permission before trying to have a child, and they must often wait a long time before it is given. The government promotes birth control with posters, radio programs, newspaper articles, and public speeches. Accidental pregnancies are usually ended by abortions.

In the late 1970s the government adopted a one-child-per-family policy. If a couple defies the government and tries to have more than one child, the penalties can be harsh. Officials may spend many hours pressuring them to end the pregnancy, and other people in the community may snub them. If they refuse to give in, they will pay higher taxes and their child may be denied access to the best schools.

The government campaign has been very successful in most parts of China. The birthrate has been halved in recent years. Unfortunately, though, this could create another problem. In the next century, there may be too few people of working age to support a large number of aged people. Managing population growth is perhaps China's most challenging problem.

## THE "BOY PREFERENCE"

An ancient and sad tradition continues in China—boys have always been preferred. In old China the reason was simple. When a girl grew up, she married and left the family. A boy, on the other hand, grew to young manhood and brought a wife into the family. Having a male child guaran-

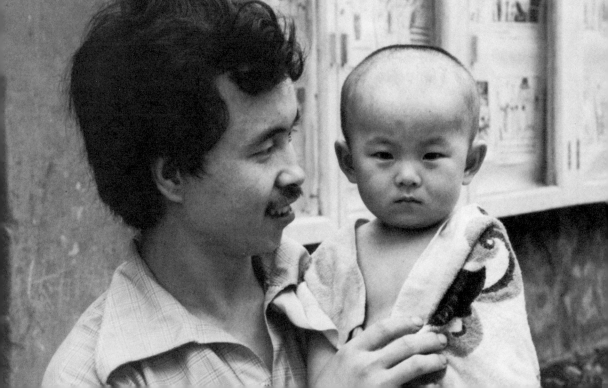

teed that his parents would have someone to care for them in their old age. In poor families, unwanted female infants were sometimes drowned or left in the open to die of exposure.

Today large colorful posters show parents and girl children with the caption: "Girls are good, too." Although the campaign seems to be working, tradition is deeply rooted in China. Occasionally infant girls are still killed in remote parts of the country.

## CARE OF THE VERY YOUNG

A Chinese mother is granted fifty-six days of maternity leave. When she returns to work, infant care is taken over by a government nursery or a grandmother living in the home.

Chinese parents and grandparents are very devoted, and children receive almost constant attention. In the late afternoon, the visitor to any city will see many families of three generations strolling in the parks. While the adults may have drab, worn clothing, the children will sport new, colorful outfits. Although many Chinese adults dislike being photographed, the visitor will rarely find a parent or grandparent unwilling to pose proudly with a child.

On a hot evening the visitor can walk past many Chinese families sitting on the sidewalks in front of their apartments. Most of the children will already be asleep in cots or in a parent's arms, unbothered by the hubbub in the street.

*Top: an old man*
*Bottom: father and child*

[55]

The adults will talk quietly and "fan their troubles away" with hand fans. There is a deep pride and tenderness in the looks they give the sleeping children. Life in China may be hard, but love for children makes the hardships easier to bear.

## MEDICAL CARE IN CHINA

Medical care is provided free or at a very low cost to all people in China. A sick person may be treated with modern Western methods or very old Chinese methods. The most famous traditional method is acupuncture. The ancient Chinese believed that a life force called Qi flowed through the body along fourteen paths. If the Qi was disturbed, the loss of balance between its negative side, the Yin, and its positive side, the Yang, caused a person to become ill. Sticking thin needles into several of 800 acupuncture points on the body would restore the balance and cure the patient.

For many years Western doctors thought acupuncture was worthless. In recent years, however, many have come to believe that it has value, especially for treating pain. Some operations in this country are now performed using acupuncture instead of anesthetic drugs. Modern research indicates that the needles affect the body's nervous system, blocking feeling from reaching the brain.

Western doctors have also gained more respect for traditional herbal medicine. Hundreds of natural herbs are sold all over China for the treatment of almost any illness. Research has shown that many of these herbal medicines work much like artificial drugs produced in laboratories.

China has a shortage of medical facilities and trained personnel, but health care today is better than ever before. New hospitals for both traditional and Western medical care are being built. Promising medical students are being sent to other countries to study the latest methods. To make up for part of the doctor shortage, the government has trained many "barefoot doctors," paramedics who treat minor illnesses and injuries in remote parts of the country.

# 8

## DAILY LIFE

China is very large, with as many different ways of life as there are different environments. Many of the national minorities preserve centuries-old life-styles and customs. Within the Han majority itself, life-styles differ greatly, depending on whether a family lives in a great city, in a rural farming district, along one of the great rivers, on the seacoast, high in the mountains, or deep in the forest. Are the parents educated professional people, factory workers, farmers, fishermen, miners, or do they follow any of a thousand other trades or professions? Does one of them belong to the Communist Party?

## POVERTY, COMFORT
## AND LUXURY

Despite the communist ideal of all sharing equally in the wealth of the nation, great differences exist in China. Farmers in the more fertile provinces of eastern China earn

more and live better than those who farm poorer land in other parts of the country. Government irrigation programs are helping many of the less-well-off farmers, but their incomes still lag far behind.

For many years city workers earned more than peasant farmers. This has now started to change. The free enterprise policies of Deng Xiaoping have raised rural living standards. Many peasants are today running small private businesses and earning more than city workers.

A good education can also mean a higher income. Scientists, technicians, and engineers are paid on a different scale than industrial workers and often earn several times as much.

Membership in the Communist Party is also an economic advantage. High party officials enjoy luxuries unknown anywhere else in China. Lesser party officials (cadres) receive salaries and bonuses that give them a total income well above the average. There are other privileges as well. The children of party cadres have an easier time getting into the best schools. Cadres can take their families to vacation resorts reserved for party members. They have access to stores, films, and books usually denied other Chinese. Although most party officials are honest, corruption is not unknown.

## LOW BUT RISING INCOMES

The Chinese family income is low. The average yearly income of a farm family is only about $120 per person. City

*A commune home*

workers can earn considerably more, but they must pay rent and buy their own food. The money goes a long way since many prices are kept low by the government. Still, there is little income left for more than necessities. The average family owns no more than its clothing, bedding, cooking pots, a few tools, and two or three prized luxuries. Little of any possible use is ever thrown away.

In the recent past, the average Chinese saved to buy "the four acquisitions": a wristwatch, a bicycle, a sewing machine, and a radio. Today the list is longer. Farm incomes have more than doubled since Deng and the pragmatists took power, and city wages are also increasing. Chinese families are now saving for tape recorders, washing machines, refrigerators, and televisions sets. Demand for these products exceeds the supply, and people must often wait a long time to buy.

Until recently almost no one in China owned a car, truck, or tractor. Privately owned vehicles are still rare, but some ambitious Chinese are buying them. A small taxi or trucking firm can provide a good income. A small tractor can help a farmer boost both his production and income.

*The People's Daily*, China's principal newspaper, today prints stories of peasants who are becoming rich. Instead of criticizing them as it would have a few years ago, it now announces: "Getting rich through labor is glorious." China's pragmatic leaders hope that allowing a few to become rich will eventually raise the living standards of all Chinese, since the less well-off will work harder with the example of the newly rich to follow.

The rich will be expected to help their poorer neighbors. Deng has made it very clear that China will not return to the "bad old days" when the rich were allowed to exploit and cheat the poor.

*Cooking noodles in a free market*

## BETTER CLOTHING

The Chinese are using their improved incomes to dress better. During Mao's rule, even dress styles were dictated by the party. Mao believed that dedication to communism should be shown by plain and uniform clothing. A Western business suit or a colorful blouse were signs of "capitalist decadence."

Today people feel more free to dress according to their tastes, but there is not the variety of everyday dress styles that we see in our country. Peasant farmers in the fields dress in dark baggy pants and blouses, much as they have for generations. White shirts and dark slacks or skirts are the usual dress for workers in the cities. High Communist officials still wear blue "Mao jackets." Yet a high Communist official may wear a Western-style business suit to a meeting with a foreign delegation. On days off, a farmer or a city worker may reach into the closet for a bright shirt.

## MORE AND BETTER FOOD

Better times are giving the Chinese more and better food. Enough food has always been a great problem in China. Since the great famine in 1960, the government has worked very hard to end the risk of starvation. The government admits that 200 million peasants are still undernourished, but the age-old fear of famine is receding.

*Mother and child*

# EATING IN CHINA

Everyday food in China is much plainer than the meals we order in American Chinese restaurants. Only the occasional banquet is as fancy. People in South China eat a great deal of rice—five or six bowls a day. Noodles are the staple in the North.

Breakfast is simple and eaten quickly. Vegetables, porridge, and steamed bread are typical ingredients. In the city, lunch is also simple—probably noodles or rice with seasonings or broth—and the main meal of the day is eaten in the evening. In the countryside, the largest meal of the day is eaten at mid-day.

A main meal in country or city will probably include vegetables, soup, rice or noodles, and a small amount of pork, chicken, duck, or fish. Meat and vegetables are cut into tiny pieces and nothing that can possibly be eaten is wasted. The food is usually steamed or stir-fried in a wok—a metal utensil whose curved sides allow a little oil to go a long way. In various parts of the country, soy sauce, vinegar, garlic, mustard, ginger, hot peppers, and scallions are often used to add flavor to the dishes. Chopsticks are used to eat the meal—a feat mastered even by the very young.

Green tea is drunk not only at mealtime but many times during the day. The Chinese view tea as far more than a drink to satisfy thirst. Tea restores a person's ability to think and work. It is also a social drink and encourages conversation. Even on the hottest day, a visitor is frequently offered a steaming cup of tea.

Since few families have refrigerators, shopping for food is a daily chore. Each family receives coupons to buy the basic necessities at government stores. Most Chinese prefer to buy other items in the free markets, where prices are not fixed and the food is fresher. The free markets are noisy, crowded, and colorful. Along the narrow street, the shopper will find huge piles of fresh vegetables, live chickens and ducks, tubs of eels, a truckload of watermelons, baskets of eggs, and dozens of other items. Many of the peasant farmers have spent most of the day pushing heavy carts or pedaling overloaded bicycles to bring their food to market.

If a banquet is planned, a Chinese wife or grandmother may spend hours shopping in the free market. When she finds an item she wants, she haggles with the farmer until a price is agreed. At home, preparations are made with great care. Banquets are used to mark special occasions. They can include a dozen or more courses and will be talked about for months afterward.

# THE LUXURY OF PRIVACY

Privacy is a luxury in much of China. In eastern China so many people occupy so little land that privacy is difficult to find. In the cities, three generations may share an apartment the size of an American living room. Adult sisters, brothers, or cousins may move in while waiting for an apartment of their own. A tremendous amount of new housing has been built in recent years, but there is still far from enough.

Outside the major cities, few homes have electricity or running water. Water is drawn from a communal tap or pump. Kerosene lamps provide light. Some of the more modern rural districts have long rows of single-story apartments. Elsewhere, peasants have individuals homes with two or three small rooms. The walls are built of mud bricks, and the few windows are often covered with paper rather than glass. In the northern provinces, the homes can be very cold in the winter. The brick beds are heated from below with pipes running from the stove.

In the city or country, several families usually share a bathroom and kitchen. Only though cooperation and patience can people accomplish routine chores. When an argument breaks out, it soon becomes a community affair. Neighbors gather to listen, offering comments and suggestions. Usually the argument is quickly settled. Tensions have been released and a little entertainment provided. Considering the crowded conditions, it is remarkable that life goes on so smoothly.

# CONFORMITY

In our society the person who does not conform is often admired as a rugged individualist. In China the nonconformist is more likely to be viewed as a troublemaker. Conformity has been considered a virtue in China since the time of Confucius. The good citizen keeps his individuality within tight limits. There is not enough space in China for over a billion rugged individualists. A phrase for the Chinese attitude entered our language during World War II, "gung ho"—"work together."

In China a person who chooses to violate the standards of conformity will be corrected. Neighbors, relatives, schoolmates, or comrades at work will talk to him or her. If this pressure produces no response, the local cadre will soon confront the person. The next step may be "public criticism," a group meeting where others loudly condemn the actions in question.

If the nonconformity becomes actual lawbreaking, the punishment can be harsh. Minor criminals risk fines, jail terms, and—worst of all—humiliation in the tight Chinese society. More serious offenders may be sent to remote camps where they are taught "the error of their ways," while working at heavy labor. Unfortunately, there are still a number of prisoners in these camps who have been guilty of nothing more than loud criticism of the Communist system.

Violent criminals may be sent to prison. Murderers, rapists, and those guilty of extreme corruption may be executed—sometimes publicly before thousands of spectators. However, the crime rate in China is low compared with that of many countries, including the United States.

*Police posters of
executed felons*

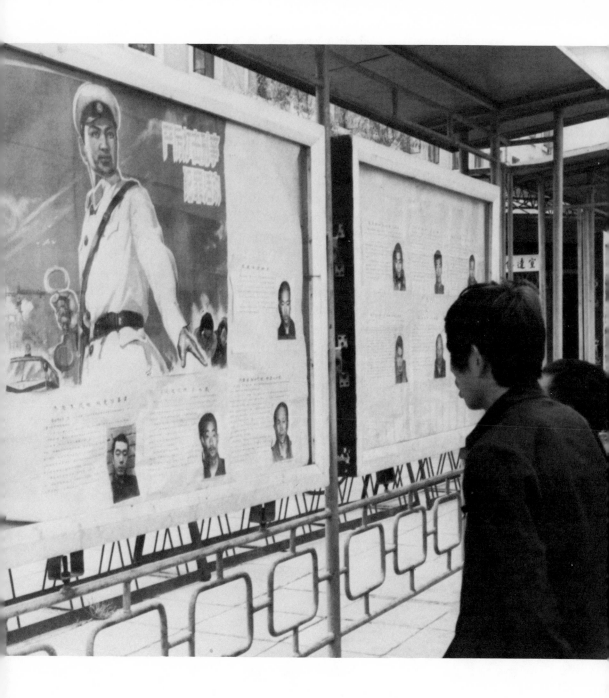

# THE EVER-PRESENT
# COMMUNIST PARTY

Communist rule has brought much good to the people of China in recent years. Widespread hunger is no longer the curse of China. Living standards are rising. At least for now, there is political stability. Women enjoy equal rights under the constitution. Education, medical care, nutrition, and housing have been greatly improved.

Communist rule has also brought some things that we would find intolerable. Civil rights are limited. The system controls many aspects of life that we expect to control for ourselves. It seems that the party in the person of one of its officials is never far away. The party orders and all but a few obey. But this, too, is changing. Deng and the pragmatists have decided that the "responsibility system" will modernize China faster than the old policies of tight government planning and control. As the Chinese gain experience and confidence in their economic choices, they are taking greater control of their personal lives. More and more, the hovering party cadre is finding him- or herself ignored.

In some ways life-styles in China have changed little in centuries. In other regards the Chinese way of life is changing rapidly and dramatically. The children of today's China are growing to adulthood in an exciting and challenging time. They will need all the skills they can master to build the China of the twenty-first century.

# 9

## GOING TO
## SCHOOL
## IN CHINA

In the late afternoon, schoolchildren seem to be everywhere in China. Knots of children in uniforms, often with red scarves around their necks, make their way along crowded city streets or narrow commune paths. They stop to giggle at the Western visitor and shout a few simple words of English. Older students shyly approach the visitor and try their conversational skills. Many speak English quite well.

At times China seems like an entire nation at school. Communist rule has made education available to everyone for the first time in China's long history. The people have responded with enthusiasm. In old China eight out of ten people were illiterate—unable to read and write. Only well-off families could afford the price of school. They sent only their sons, daughters staying home to learn domestic skills. Today almost all young people in China receive an education, and many adults attend night classes.

## KINDERGARTENS

Many Chinese children start kindergarten at the age of three; others stay home with a grandmother. Kindergartens usually hold classes five and a half days a week. Six subjects are taught: art, language, physical education, music, arithmetic, and general studies.

Kindergartens are lively places. The children are encouraged to enjoy learning and, like all children, they can be very noisy. They are taught very young to work together and to be good school citizens. There is rarely any fighting or crying. When the teacher calls for attention, the children are quickly quiet.

Many Chinese kindergartens are boarding schools, where the children live during the week. They sleep in long rows of cribs and cots. The children are picked up by their parents on Saturday afternoon and returned to school on Monday morning.

A typical kindergarten has 300 to 400 students and 20 teachers. Each teacher is likely to have one or two aides. Another 30 or so adults work around the school.

## ELEMENTARY SCHOOLS

At six or seven, a child starts elementary school. School life is now more serious and students are expected to work

*Top: kindergarten children in a music class*
*Bottom: students in a high school classroom*

hard. The school day begins at 7:30 and ends at 4:00, with a break for lunch between 11:40 and 2:00. (Long lunch hours are traditional in China, although that, too, is changing.) Courses include science, mathematics, history, physical education, Chinese, art, crafts, music, and often English.

Buildings are frequently old, sometimes converted warehouses or factories. A typical class will have forty or more students, and conditions are usually crowded. The lighting is often poor, and rural schools in the south may be open-air with no glass or screens in the windows. Individual desks are rare and students often sit three or four to a bench, working on a table in front of them.

Working together is encouraged. Better students help their classmates. Physical education classes emphasize team sports, relay races, and group exercises. Homework is assigned and parents are expected to supervise its completion. Some schools require parents to sign the homework.

Schools have sports teams, clubs, and other extracurricular activities. Typical activities include volleyball, basketball, table tennis, singing and dancing, instrumental music, handicrafts, stamp collecting, photography, electronics, and scholarly competitions.

Schools have simple citizenship codes that students are expected to learn. The Four Modernizations are often mentioned. Other principles include: Love the People; Love the Old; Love the Motherland. Many schools have incentive programs to reward good citizenship and performance. Students who do well in their studies and perform good deeds are rewarded with prizes or taken on special field trips.

Education does not end at the close of the school day. Many cities have "children's palaces." In these recreational buildings, children can follow their own interests in studying a skill or developing a hobby. Teachers organize activities that are both fun and educational.

### LEARNING TO
### WRITE CHINESE

Children entering school in China have a difficult task before them: learning to write their language. Chinese has at least 50,000 characters. Fortunately, no one has to know all of them. About 6,000 are commonly used. To read a newspaper a person must learn as many as 4,000 characters.

Our alphabet is phonetic with each of the twenty-six letters representing a sound. Chinese characters are ideographs representing ideas. By combining different Chinese characters, different ideas can be expressed. For example:

the character "speak" 説

and
the character "bright" 明

together mean "explanation." 説　明

Calligraphy, beautiful handwriting with brushes and ink, is an ancient art in China. Some people study all their lives to give just the right flourish to their handwriting.

Literacy is particularly valuable in China because the pronunciation of Chinese varies widely. People from different parts of the country may not understand each other's spoken words, but they can communicate through the universal written language.

To ease the problems of learning Chinese, the government has simplified about 3,000 of the most commonly used characters. All schools in China now teach the pronunciation of the Beijing dialect. Eventually, the government hopes, people all over China will be able to communicate easily in both written and spoken Chinese.

## EXAMINATIONS

Yearly exams begin in elementary school. The most important exam is taken at the end of the sixth grade, and a student must pass it before continuing on to secondary school. Examinations become increasingly important in the next few years. The student who hopes eventually to have a very good job must do better and better as the competition increases.

## SECONDARY SCHOOL

Many less able students begin to work part-time at about thirteen, while attending vocational schools half days. More than half of all students leave school for jobs before completing the full six years of secondary school. The best students continue to study a broad range of subjects. Competition is intense, since only about ten of every hundred high school graduates can win places in universities and technical colleges.

## HIGHER EDUCATION

Chinese universities have been rebuilt since the chaos of the Cultural Revolution. Higher education is once again respected in China, and it is no longer bad to be an "intellectual."

College students are willing to work very hard. A college degree means better pay, more interesting work, better working conditions, and more privileges. However, earning a degree is not easy. The hours spent in class and studying are long. Often six students live in a room smaller than a dormitory room for two on an American campus.

Hurried meals are often eaten standing up at small round tables in a busy cafeteria.

China is showing renewed interest in learning modern skills from the West. Some of the very best students are sent to study in other countries. They are usually greatly surprised by the freedoms and opportunities available in a democracy. Often they return home very different people. Many of China's future leaders will come from among these elite students. No one knows how they will use their experiences to reshape China.

## CHOICE OF CAREERS

One of the major complaints of high school and college students in China today is their lack of choice in education and careers. Students can express their wishes, but the government decides what the nation needs; students are directed to prepare for those jobs. To make matters worse, the government has not been good at the task and many high school and college students find themselves without jobs on graduation. Some may wait for work as long as two years and then receive assignments that do not match their educations. Some assignments may send them far from home. It is difficult to change jobs, and the complainer risks damaging his or her career.

## ADULT EDUCATION

Since the Communists came to power in 1949, the government has made a tremendous effort to teach everyone to read and write. Even very old people have gone to school for the first time in their lives. Today a majority of Chinese are literate. The government continues to push adult education. Those who missed a good education during the Cultural Revolution are encouraged to attend night-school classes. Teachers are sent into remote areas to hold classes for nomads. Television and radio stations provide a large number of educational programs.

The Chinese leaders know that to build a modern China, the country must have an educated populace. Today, though the Chinese educational system is better than ever before, there are still problems. Buildings and laboratories are old. Money is short. Universities do not have enough first-rate professors. China's schools have not produced enough technicians and professional people in some fields, while other fields have too many. Yet the government's commitment is strong, and the Chinese people are eager for education.

# 10

## WORK AND
## RECREATION

The hill is steep and the load of concrete blocks is heavy. At the front of the cart, three men are bent almost double with the strain of pulling on the ropes running from the cart to the harnesses across their narrow chests. At the back of the cart, three more men push, grunting with exertion. A Western visitor on the sidewalk watches in awe, then shakes his head. "You've got to be tough in this country," he says to a companion.

Work is terribly hard in China. Nowhere in the world are so many loads moved, so many fields plowed, and so many ditches dug with raw muscle. Little amazes the Western visitor so much as the primitive technology in China. Wooden plows, hoes, rakes, barrels, and wheelbarrows; woven baskets, mats, and fences; pottery jars from small to huge—these are the age-old tools and utensils of the Chinese peasants. Horses, donkeys, and water buffalo are more likely to be their companions in the fields and on the roads than tractors or trucks.

All across China the visitor sees incredible feats of strength, endurance, and ingenuity. Peasant men and women trot along paths, balancing awkward loads on either end of shoulder poles—baskets of earth, bales of grass, bound pigs, baskets of live chickens and ducks, even small children too tired to walk farther on the long way home. Down the narrow roads come bicycles loaded so high with produce that the pedalers' balancing acts could fit in a circus. Wheelbarrows and carts carry everything—bricks for new homes, coal for cooking fires, fodder for the animals, human waste to fertilize the fields, farm produce bound for a nearby free market, fat pigs going to slaughter—the list is endless.

This is China at work: a land of great toil done with primitive tools; a land striving with muscle and grit to pull itself into the twentieth century and beyond. The large majority of Chinese are farmers. Most of their farming tools and methods have gone unchanged for hundreds, even thousands, of years. When the Chinese leaders speak of the modernization of agriculture, they are talking about a task so huge it staggers the imagination. More trucks, tractors, and other modern machinery will help. The increased independence being given farmers will help. Yet China is so large that it will be decades before the age-old methods can be put completely aside.

*Without modern tools,*
*workers strain to move*
*a concrete floor slab.*

# THE "RICE BOWL"

In old China, a person's "rice bowl" was his way of making a living. "Rice bowls" were handed down from generation to generation. If a father was a farmer, a shoemaker, or a mandarin, it was likely that his son would have the same livelihood or profession. A very bright peasant lad could in theory become a mandarin, but in reality very few could afford the education. Another lad might escape to the city to become a rickshaw puller, but he, too, would be the rare exception. For young women the future was even more limited, their roles fixed by iron tradition.

Today the situation is better. Education is now available to everyone; women have equality—at least on paper. With determination, intelligence, and luck, some young people are able to escape the hard life of their parents. The vast majority, however, still inherit the "rice bowl."

# ESCAPING TO THE CITY

Many ambitious young people want to escape from the countryside to a big city—especially Beijing, Shanghai, or Guangzhou. In the cities there are more opportunities: wages are higher; recreational opportunities are greater; modern conveniences are easier to buy; members of the opposite sex are easier to meet. In the cities one can "get

*Top: "Following his long shadow home."*
*This form of transportation is the*
*rule, not the exception. Bottom:*
*young women in a clothing factory.*

ahead." But without the permission of the government, no one can move from the countryside.

Jobs in China are assigned by the government and are usually held for life. The young particularly resent the lack of freedom in choosing and changing jobs. They call the government policy the "iron rice bowl." Deng Xiaoping and China's pragmatic leaders have recently loosened some of the rules. It is now becoming easier for people to change jobs or start their own small businesses. Yet most people must still "eat from the iron rice bowl."

## WORKING IN THE CITY

The newcomer to the city is unlikely to find his or her new job much easier than working in the countryside. Construction crews and workers in such heavy industries as steel making have dirty, hard, and frequently dangerous jobs. Here, too, human muscle is used more often than modern machinery.

Workers in light industries such as clothing or pottery manufacture have easier but by no means comfortable jobs. Factories are often almost unbearably hot; lighting and ventilation are often poor. Long rows of workers, usually women, bend to their tasks for long hours, five and a half or six days a week. In all industries there are quotas to be met and little time to relax.

China's leaders are introducing more free enterprise in the cities. Small independent businesses are springing up. Factories are now allowed to set their own quotas, compete with other factories, and distribute more of the profits to the workers. After years of trying to modernize heavy industry, the government is concentrating on light industries. Consumer goods like televisions, radios, and wristwatches are pouring out of Chinese factories.

China's pragmatic leaders know that industrial modernization will be almost as difficult as agricultural modernization. They are increasingly seeking help from abroad. Modern machines and even entire factories are being bought. China is seeking loans from foreign banks to help finance these purchases. Special economic zones have been set up in coastal provinces to attract foreign investment. Deng recently said, "No country can now develop by closing its door." This is a major change in the attitude of Chinese leaders.

## ENJOYING THE HOURS OFF

Because hard work fills so much of their lives, the Chinese take particular joy in their hours off. Their pleasures are usually simple by our standards, but they are enjoyed to the fullest.

The Chinese are nature lovers. A brief vacation trip to one of the nation's many natural wonders or historic sites is an event to be planned months in advance and its memory enjoyed for months after. China's many city parks are so heavily used that not all Chinese can be given the same days off. Many workers labor through the weekend and receive their time off during the week.

Parks provide a place for the Chinese to engage in their passion for sports. In the early morning, usually well before 6:00, hundreds will gather in the parks to exercise in groups or by themselves. Taijiquan [tai-gi-chuan], the ancient "shadowboxing," is popular, particularly with older people. Years of practice and intense concentration are required to master the slow, rhythmic pattern of the exercise. It looks easy and hardly taxing, but it leaves a person sweating. Watching an old man perform taijiquan may be his pet, a caged songbird taken out for its morning "exercise."

Younger people usually prefer more active exercises than taijiquan. Many jog in the morning or play team sports like soccer, volleyball, and basketball in the evening. Also popular is a ballet of mock combat performed with unsharpened swords and spears. In groups or individually against invisible opponents, participants run and leap high in the air. They swing their weapons while performing difficult aerial gynmastics. It is beautiful to watch.

## MOVIES, CONCERTS, AND PLAYS

The Chinese have a rich heritage in the performing arts. During the Cultural Revolution, traditional music and drama were replaced by "revolutionary" plays, songs, and movies. The people were quickly bored and avoided the performances. Today traditional performances are again allowed and theaters and movie houses are packed. The buildings are usually old, the ventilation poor, and the seats hard, but nothing dampens the enthusiam of the audience. In the countryside, touring companies often perform out of doors.

Plays usually retell a familar story from Chinese folklore or history. The costumes are beautiful. The singing is high-pitched and unfamilar to Western ears, but it is flawlessly performed. Dancing and juggling are frequently part of a performance.

The government is again allowing some foreign films to be shown. Charlie Chaplin's silent comedies were recently the rage. More recent films are also shown, although the government still censors many of them to protect China from "cultural pollution."

Artists are feeling freer to express their ideas. Only a few years ago, they could write or paint about few subjects except the glory of Mao and the revolution. But the artists are still cautious; many of them spent too much time in rural exile to forget quickly.

## READING

The Chinese are enthusiastic readers. For a few pennies a reader can rent a book from one of the many sidewalk bookstands and join the crowd of other readers sitting nearby. During the Cultural Revolution, the "little red book" containing quotations from the thought of Mao Zedong was required reading. Today practical books on self-help and advancement hold most interest for ambitious young people. Those looking for more relaxing fare may choose one of the many thick comic books on the stands. More books and magazines from other countries are now appearing on sidewalk bookstands.

## SIMPLE PLEASURES

Simple evening pleasures are as old as China itself. Walking down a quiet neighborhood lane at dusk, we find people enjoying the peaceful time at the end of the long day. Men and women talk, joke, or simply "fan their troubles away" in the warm evening. A few children are still awake, sleepily playing near proud parents and grandparents. Two or three radios can be heard, but they play the ancient music of China softly; it is the quiet time and a good citizen keeps the volume low.

Around a small table, several men play a card game. Two other men sit cross-legged on the ground, concentrating on a game of Chinese chess. Small groups watch both games. One of the card players looks up and gently kids a nephew. The young man is going to a dance, until recently a forbidden pleasure. The uncle knows his nephew desperately wants to meet the "right" girl, and he wishes him luck.

Two older men, returning from a nearby teahouse, stop to exchange the news of the day with spectators. They have been drinking tea and talking with old friends. Their evening has been calm and peaceful, and now they go in for a late supper.

A few doors farther on a small crowd is watching the new television set bought by a young couple after many months of saving and waiting. The young husband and wife stand by proudly, happy to share their good fortune.

On this quiet street, there is a feeling of community: a sense of shared suffering and happiness that is an eternal part of the Chinese spirit. Together these neighbors share a sense of old China's greatness and humiliation, of the struggle and turmoil since the revolution, of the risk and promise of the future.

The television announcer is describing recent progress on the great dam at Yichang. The camera slowly pans across a night scene—a forest of brightly lighted cranes and tumbling streams of welding sparks. For the watchers the dam and the television set itself are evidence that modernization is coming to China—slowly and with great toil, but as inevitably as the mighty Yangtze flows to the sea.

# TO LEARN
# MORE
# ABOUT CHINA

Boase, Wendy. *Early China.* New York: Gloucester Press, 1978.

Hughes-Stanton, Penelope. *See Inside an Ancient Chinese Town.* New York: Franklin Watts, 1979.

Knox, Robert. *Ancient China.* New York: Warwick Press, 1979.

Loescher, Gil, with Ann Dull Loescher. *China: Pushing Toward the Year 2000.* New York: Harcourt Brace Jovanovich, 1981.

McLenighan, Valjean. *China: A History to 1949.* Chicago: Children's Press, 1983.

National Geographic Society. *Journey into China.* Washington, D.C.: 1982.

Poole, Frederick King. *Mao Zedong.* New York: Franklin Watts, 1982.

———. *An Album of Modern China.* New York: Franklin Watts, 1981.

# INDEX